Sebastian Diemer

Does money matter in predicting future events?

Anchor Compact

Diemer, Sebastian: Does money matter in predicting future events?
Hamburg, Anchor Academic Publishing 2013
Original title of the thesis: Real-Money vs. Play-Money Forecasting Accuracy in Online Prediction Markets

Buch-ISBN: 978-3-95489-132-0
PDF-eBook-ISBN: 978-3-95489-632-5
Druck/Herstellung: Anchor Academic Publishing, Hamburg, 2013
Additionally: London, London School of Economics, England

Bibliografische Information der Deutschen Nationalbibliothek:
Die Deutsche Nationalbibliothek verzeichnet diese Publikation in der Deutschen Nationalbibliografie; detaillierte bibliografische Daten sind im Internet über http://dnb.d-nb.de abrufbar

Bibliographical Information of the German National Library:
The German National Library lists this publication in the German National Bibliography. Detailed bibliographic data can be found at: http://dnb.d-nb.de

All rights reserved. This publication may not be reproduced, stored in a retrieval system or transmitted, in any form or by any means, electronic, mechanical, photocopying, recording or otherwise, without the prior permission of the publishers.

Das Werk einschließlich aller seiner Teile ist urheberrechtlich geschützt. Jede Verwertung außerhalb der Grenzen des Urheberrechtsgesetzes ist ohne Zustimmung des Verlages unzulässig und strafbar. Dies gilt insbesondere für Vervielfältigungen, Übersetzungen, Mikroverfilmungen und die Einspeicherung und Bearbeitung in elektronischen Systemen.

Die Wiedergabe von Gebrauchsnamen, Handelsnamen, Warenbezeichnungen usw. in diesem Werk berechtigt auch ohne besondere Kennzeichnung nicht zu der Annahme, dass solche Namen im Sinne der Warenzeichen- und Markenschutz-Gesetzgebung als frei zu betrachten wären und daher von jedermann benutzt werden dürften.

Die Informationen in diesem Werk wurden mit Sorgfalt erarbeitet. Dennoch können Fehler nicht vollständig ausgeschlossen werden und die Diplomica Verlag GmbH, die Autoren oder Übersetzer übernehmen keine juristische Verantwortung oder irgendeine Haftung für evtl. verbliebene fehlerhafte Angaben und deren Folgen.

Alle Rechte vorbehalten

© Anchor Academic Publishing, ein Imprint der Diplomica® Verlag GmbH
http://www.diplom.de, Hamburg 2013
Printed in Germany

Abstract

Prediction markets are online trading platforms where contracts on future events are traded with payoffs being exclusively linked to event occurrence. Scientific research has shown that market prices of such contracts imply high forecasting accuracy through effective information aggregation of dispersed knowledge. This phenomenon is related to incentives for truthful aggregation in the form of real-money or play-money rewards. The question whether real- or play-money incentives enhance higher relative forecast accuracy has been addressed by previous works with diverse findings. The current state of empirical research in his field is subject to two inherent deficiencies. First, inter-market studies suffer from market disparities and differences in the definition of underlying events. Comparisons between two different platforms (one for play-money contracts, one for real-money contracts) are potentially biased by different trading behaviour. Second, the majority of studies are based upon identical datasets of market platforms (IOWA stock exchange, Tradesports/Intrade, NewsFutures).

This thesis contributes new insights by analysing 44,169 trading observations on ipredict, where real-money and play-money contracts are traded on a variety of events. Forecasting accuracy is analysed on overall trading activity as well as comparison of equal contracts under different monetary incentive schemes. Statistical models are built to analyse the influence of order volumes and days to expiry under both incentive schemes. Ignoring different events in underlying trading activity, play-money contracts imply statistically insignificant excess accuracy. In direct comparison of equal events, real-money contracts, however, real-money contracts predict at significantly higher accuracy. This thesis finds a relationship between order volumes and forecasting accuracy whereas the influence of days to expiry and aggregated volumes showed lower R^2 than was expected by formed hypotheses.

List of Content

1. Introduction and Theoretical Fundamentals 1
  1.1   Introduction 1
  1.2   Definition of Prediction Markets 2
  1.3   Theoretical Framework 3

2. Literature Overview 7
  2.1   Real-money vs. Play-money 7
  2.2   Other Factors With Influence on Forecasting Accuracy 8
  2.3   Closed Prediction Markets 9

3. Data 11
  3.1   Data Provider 11
  3.2   Definition of Variables 14

4. Results 17
  4.1   Overall Data 17
  4.2   Real-Money vs. Play-Money: Portfolio Comparison 18
  4.3   Real-Money vs. Play-Money: Direct Contract Comparison 22
  4.4   Real-Money /Play-Money: Influencing Factors 24
  4.5   Conclusion 25

References 27

Appendix 30

1. Introduction and Theoretical Fundamentals

1.1 Introduction

Sir Francis Galton discovered the phenomenon of crowd wisdom by studying submitted guesses from a public wager in 1906. A monetary price was awarded to the individual who most accurately estimated the weight of an exposed ox. By computing the mean and median of all 800 submitted guesses, he found that the mean showed a spread of mere 1 pound to the ex-post determined slaughtering weight (Surowiecki, 2004). Although no guess equalled the determined weight, crowds collectively predicted at much higher accuracy than the individual.

This simple principle of providing monetary incentives for truthful revelation and aggregation of dispersed knowledge still constitutes the underlying concept of modern prediction markets (they are also referred to as virtual stock markets, information markets, idea futures or forecasting markets). In recent year, political, economic, and academic interest in such market platforms has risen tremendously:

The United States' Defense Advanced Research Projects Agency launched a prediction market (Policy Analysis Market) in 2003 on political and economic events in the middle-east (Polk et al., 2003) to gain knowledge on future events. The project became politically instrumentalized and therefore was abandoned after a short period of time. Since then, private companies have utilized the economic potential and generate billions in trading volume (betfair.com) despite legal bans in many jurisdictions. Table 1 provides an overview of today's large-scale international prediction markets. Platforms on which virtual money instead of real-money is traded have likewise grown in number and scale in the form of corporate planning tools as well as skill-based online gaming applications.

Academic interest focuses on the market prices of such platforms, which can be interpreted as probability of occurrence for underlying events. Implicit predictions have proven to yield accurate results on all kinds of future events (particularly political elections) under both incentive schemes.

This thesis aims to analyse whether forecasting performance in online prediction markets differs between real- and play-money: Do contracts on real-money predict better on a systematic level (irrelevant of underlying events) and how do equal contracts compare? What other factors influence forecasting accuracy?

These questions will be stressed against a novel dataset which has not yet been studied. Real-money data is drawn from public trading information on ipredict.co.nz, play-money data was collected in a closed play-money market operated by ipredict open to finance students between March and May 2009 under equal circumstances as the real-money platform[1].

The remainder of the paper is subdivided in four consecutive parts. This section introduces a theoretical framework on the underlying concepts of prediction markets. Specifically, it will outline why market prices equal probabilities of occurrence and imply general implications on trading behaviour. Section 2 discusses findings of previous studies and consolidates these into a current state of research. The third part defines the underlying dataset and relevant variables. Empirical results are discussed in section four. Descriptive statistics, interval and regression results are discussed on a portfolio level and in direct contract comparison.

1.2 Definition of Prediction Markets

Prediction Markets can be defined as markets for future events. Such platforms make it possible to obtain, aggregate and process information of dispersed knowledge. Two different contract categories require differentiation: binary (reveal probabilities of occurrence) and indexed (reveal mean values of the underlying index). Both payoff types are present in the analysed dataset of this study.

Binary contracts are stocks tied to events that either occur or do not occur at a specific date or time interval. Contracts pay off $1 (or $10, $100, respectively) in case an event happens, zero otherwise. A hypothetical example for a contract is whether or not the United Nations will impose additional sanctions against Iran before 31.12.2010, paying off $1 if the event occurs according to predefined sources within this interval; zero if it does not. A market price of $0.67 suggests that the last trading occurrence between traders implies a 67% probability of occurrence. Market prices are sometimes misinterpreted, as market prices above 0.50 (e.g. π_1 =0.67) are falsely construed to forecast that the event will definitely occur. The sound interpretation, however, is that for 100 repetitions of the event, the event occurs 67 times. Section 1.2 explains the mechanics behind the interpretation of market prices as probabilities.

---

[1] This includes market maker settings, contract specifications, terms of use, etc.

Indexed contracts pay out the corresponding value of an underlying indicator (e.g. stock prices, interest rates, exchange rates, GDP, industry-specific data, etc.) at a specific date or the mean over a specific range, respectively. A contract paying off $1 for each rounded thousand-digit of the Dow Jones Industrial Index at 31.12.2010 is an example for an indexedcontract/event. Assuming a value of 12,230 at expiry date this contract would pay off $12. The ex-ante market value (e.g. $8.71) reveals the market's mean value of what the market believes that value will be upon expiry.

1.3 Theoretical Framework

The basic principle why market dynamics obtain and aggregate information more efficiently than centralized forecasts dates back to Hayek (1945) who discovered that a market mechanism in general performs better in revealing dispersed (asymmetric) knowledge among traders than centralized coordination. The following model shows that, regardless of the incentive structure design, market prices reflect the equilibrium in traded beliefs and can thus be interpreted as a probability of occurrence (Manski, 2004 ; Wolfers & Zitzewitz, 2006a). The model is limited to binary events, however, indexed contracts show similar trading characteristics for mean beliefs.

Binary events which are expected to occur (expiry value: $1) are denoted by π_1, the counter event (expiry value: $0) is stated as π_0, where $\pi_1 + \pi_0 = 1$. The total number of participating traders equals T, of which each individual t is subject to a different individual information signal. This heterogeneity in information signals leads to different subjective beliefs (probabilities) for each contract, stated by q_{t1}. The assumptions of equally distributed initial wealth endowments, or trading funds, denoted by (Yi) and independency of the subjective probability from π_1 yields a distribution of beliefs and endowment of P (q_1, Y). In relation to the market price π_1 rational traders buy contracts from the market whenever $q_1 > \pi_1$ and short-sell stock whenever $q_1 < \pi_1$. Implicitly, Y/ π_1 or Y/π_0 yields the number of contracts traded. It follows that the aggregated demand for contract, denoted by x, equals:

[1] $x = 1/\pi_1 * E[y(q_1 > \pi_1)]$

and supply equals

[2] $x = 1/\pi_0 * E[y(q_1 < \pi_1)]$

As the number of contracts held by each trader is a function of wealth endowment Y, the supply for contract, equals E(Y). Implicitly, the equilibrium only holds if demand equals supply:

[3] $E(y) = (1/\pi_1) * E[y * (q_1 > \pi_1)] = (1/\pi_0) * E[y * 1(q_1 < \pi_1)]$

Manski (2004) further assumes statistical independence between y and q_1 which simplifies the equation to

[4] $1 = (1/\pi_1) * P(q_1 > \pi_1) = (1/\pi_0) * P(q_1 < \pi_1)$

Under the assumption of continuous $P(q_1)$ equation [4] transforms into

[5] $1 = P(q_1 > \pi_1) + P(q_1 < \pi_1)$

Equation [5] yields the non-arbitrage condition for the trading beliefs of other traders. This model demonstrates theoretical expectations on how rational traders behave.
In situations where $q_1 = \pi_1$ (e.g. trader t believes there is a 67% chance that the UN will impose additional sanctions at a market price of $0.67), no trade occurs. A higher spread between q_1 and π_1 increases demand/supply as the market price is perceived to be mispriced based on the individual information set available to all t. Heterogeneity in beliefs therefore increases the trading volume in terms of quantity, or number of traded contracts.

Wolfers and Zitzewitz (2006) based their model on the first draft of Manski's study and showed that market prices further reflect the equilibrium of maximized individual's logarithmic utilities. The simple form of the model is tied to two additional simplifying assumptions:
Logarithmic utility functions: Demand and supply of traders are linear functions of each trader's beliefs. This excludes alternative types of risk-tolerance and fixed betting amounts per trader limiting the number of contracts. Since this very limitation

is a common feature on online play-money prediction markets the influences of relaxing this assumption are discussed in section 4.

Changes in Y are only caused by contract payoffs: If the only factor causing ΔY is the event itself, hedging-motivated trading activity of contracts is excluded. Hedging refers to trading motives based on other investments (e.g. hedging a short oil-futures position by buying contracts that Iran will be sanctioned, in expectation that this offsets losses from a rising oil price through the futures) or direct consequences from the event itself (e.g. Iranian oil facing the danger of becoming subject to export embargos – hedging by buying contracts in a prediction market). This limitation also involves the possibility to change Y by depositing or withdrawing money from the trading account.

In consideration of these assumptions, for all traders the number of contracts bought/sold becomes subject to the following maximization equation:

[6] $\quad \max U_j = q_j \log [y + x_j (1 - \pi_1)] + (1-q_j) \log [y - x_j \pi_1]$

[7] $\quad x_j^* = y \frac{q-\pi}{\pi(1-\pi)}$

The market price is in equilibrium when aggregated supply equals aggregated demand:

[8] $\quad \int_{-\infty}^{\pi} y \frac{q-\pi}{\pi(1-\pi)} f(q) dq = \int_{\pi}^{\infty} y \frac{\pi-q}{\pi(1-\pi)} f(q) dq$

Further, assuming no correlation between (q) and (Y) [8] simplifies to:

[9] $\quad \frac{y}{\pi(1-\pi)} \int_{-\infty}^{\pi} (q - \pi) f(q) dq = \frac{y}{\pi(1-\pi)} \int_{-\pi}^{\infty} (\pi - q) f(q) dq$

and to:

[10] $\quad \pi = \int_{-\infty}^{\infty} q f(q) dq = \bar{q}$

As shown in the previous model, heterogeneity in beliefs and high wealth endowments have most influence on market price movements, as trading activity of rational traders is determined by the factors q (subjective beliefs), π (market prices), Y (wealth endowment) and risk aversion.

This yields implications relevant for the further scope of this thesis on how trading activity depends on the following factors: incentives for revelation, changes in wealth, and risk-tolerance. For increasing spreads between q and π and a given wealth endowment (Y) the number of supplied/demanded contracts increases. In a scenario where all traders hold identical beliefs relative to the current market price, no trading activity occurs. Hence, trading volume is sensitive to diversity in information signals and the willingness to reveal this perceived mispricing truthfully. Monetary rewards or punishment, respectively, are the underlying factors that lead prediction markets to aggregate information at higher accuracy than forecasting methods that do not offer analogue incentives schemes (surveys, polls). It is valid to derive the assumption that real-money markets create more severe incentives for revelation as real-money incentives show greater influence on individual utilities.

Higher wealth endowments at a given spread between market price and individual beliefs also has a positive influence on the number of contracts an individual is willing to trade. Any change in Y is either related to individuals depositing/withdrawing funds, payoffs from expiring contracts or buying/selling activity in active contracts. For incentive purposes, most play-money markets equip users with initial wealth endowment that only changes through trading activity and exclude the possibility to deposit/withdraw funds. Real-money platforms, on the other hand, allow changes in Y that are not related to trading activity through depositing/withdrawing funds from/to an external bank account. Assuming risk-averse trading behaviour, market prices at greater uncertainty (π close to 0.50) yield higher risk and are thus expected to generate lower trading volumes than contracts showing low levels of risk. (π close to expiry value as uncertainty about the outcome of the event diminishes). Therefore, as contracts approach expiry values ($1 or $0, respectively) trading volumes are expected to escalate under both incentive types in terms of number of observed trades. Assumed risk-averseness further leads to the expectation of low $ volumes in such trades since trading activity is motivated by low-risk trading gains rather than excess information about the event.

2. Literature Overview

Tziralis and Tatsiopoulos (2007) provide an overview of academic material on prediction markets between 1991 and 2006. Overall, 152 articles have been published with a rapid growth in number observable over recent years (Figure 1). This rich body of academic literature has agreed on the accuracy of prediction markets relative to alternative forecasting methods in political and sport related contracts (Berg et al., 1996; 2008a; 2008b; Pennock et al., 2001; Spann & Skiera, 2009).

2.1 Real-Money vs. Play-Money

Servan-Schreiber et al. (2004) analysed the forecast accuracy of real-money contracts (Tradesports.com), play-money contracts (Newsfutures.com) and experts trading probabilities (propabilityfootball.com) in 208 NFL games between September and December 2003. By taking the pre-game market price (markets were closed as soon as the sports event started) of these games 416 observations were analysed (208 are independent variables since $\pi_1 + \pi_0 = 1$). The average forecast errors equal 0.439 for real-money markets and 0.436 for play-money markets. At a 90% confidence level both types of prediction markets performed better than the probability trading platform. Notably, real-money markets did not demonstrate higher forecast accuracy than play-money markets: "[...] prediction markets based on play money can be just as accurate as those based on real money" (Servan-Schreiber et al., 2004, p.250). The underlying dataset consisted of identical contracts in sports events from different platforms. Whether or not the non-existing spread was solely determined the incentive structures remained an open question.

Rosenbloom & Notz (2006) applied a Sequential Probability Ratio Test to sports (NFL 2003 season – North American team sports) and economic events (Dow Jones forecasts in 2004). Like the previously described paper, both events were traded as binary contracts on Tradesports.com and Newsfutures.com.

Again, no statistically significant spread in forecast accuracy between real- and play-money was observable for sport related contracts. For economic events, on the contrary, real-money did exhibit statistically significant (on a 5% level) higher forecast accuracy than play-money trading. Rosenbloom and Notz (2006, p.69) concluded:

> *"a closer look at the data strongly suggests that the results are market related [...] We can only speculate on why there might be differences between popular sports events and other events [...] Indeed, both effects may have occurred and only additional research, probably experimental, can address this issue successfully."*

Since no subsequent work addressed this very question, two fundamental questions are left open for additional research:

First, does real-money generate better forecasting accuracy regardless of the market type and applied methodology? Since results were found to be market-related, additional research of real-money and play-money contracts traded under equal external market circumstances is required.

Second, is the spread in accuracy related to contract categories or single contract specifics? Whereas no effect was found in sports-related contracts, economic events showed significance. This spread can either be inherent in the category (is play-money a proper incentive for sports events but not for economic-related contracts) or to the specific nature of contracts (e.g. higher uncertainty for sports events, which cannot be compensated for by efficient incentive schemes).

2.2 Other Factors With Influence on Forecasting Accuracy

Luckner (2008) discusses relevant studies based on various online platforms. Berg et al. (2000) consolidate findings of empirical studies on the IOWA prediction market, a prediction platform on political elections which has been operating since 1988. The study is limited to political, indexed contracts which pay off $1 for each per cent of votes or allocated seats a specific political party achieves in US or foreign elections. The dataset included 5 markets for presidential elections, 14 markets for other elections and 30 markets for non-US elections. A total of 237 predictions in 49 markets generated average forecast errors of 0.0137 for US elections, 0.043 for other US elections and 0.012 for non-US elections. The significant spread in overall forecast accuracy compared to the findings of Servan-Schreiber et al. (2004) and Rosenbloom and Notz (2006) is inherently tied to market factors (market maker, fees, deposit limits, etc.), contract design (sports/politics, binary/indexed) and market dynamics (trading volumes, quality of predictions, behavioural aspects).

A further study on the IOWA prediction market by Berg, Forsythe and Rietz (1996) reveals significant aspects about influencing factors on the variance of forecast errors.

Firstly, quantity (volume of trades) showed a significant positive influence on forecast accuracy. Forsythe, Rietz and Ross (1999) on the other hand, found highly accurate forecasting for small-scale laboratory based experiments. Likewise, Smith (1982) states that a number of individuals exposed to private information signals are sufficient for market efficiency. This calls into question whether trading volumes in fact influence forecast accuracy or whether high quality predictions can compensate for lower quantities. Second, some contract categories (presidential elections) attracted higher trading volumes than others. Third, trading activity grew in number and volume as contracts approached expiry. This finding supports the risk-averse nature of trading activity discussed above.

Arrow et al. (2008) postulates forecast accuracy to be dependent on days until expiry for contracts on the IOWA prediction market. Whereas volatility did not decrease substantially, trading prices tended to fluctuate more closely around the ex-post value as more information was available to trading individuals. However, this interpretation is based on a graphical interpretation of a linear relationship and lacks quantification.

2.3 Closed Prediction Markets

Closed prediction markets are limited to individuals meeting certain criteria (e.g. employees of specific company, students of a certain university) or are limited to certain physical environments (e.g. laboratory, office space).

Since the dataset studied in this paper was partly obtained through trading in a closed market environment, discussion is required whether markets with a limited number of participants have the same potential in forecasting accuracy as open ones.

Closed prediction markets aggregate information held by a comparably small number of individuals in possession of private information signals. Companies have successfully implemented closed prediction markets for sales forecasts, project management and R&D processes in recent years (Ivanov, 2009). These markets are usually operated as play-money markets implemented by third-party vendors. Besides Google, Hewlett Packard, Nokia, Motorola, Microsoft, Intel, Best Buy, Chrysler and have implemented internal markets (Cowgill et al, 2008 ; Wolfers & Zitzewitz, 2006b). Chen and Plott (2009) found sales forecasts generated by the closed HP market to be more accurate than figures by a central corporate planning unit. However, it is unclear whether the predictions within this market would have been more accurate when being traded in an open market. Does a small number of participants predict as well as an unlimited body of individuals? Does the higher amount of expertise knowledge compensate the lower degree of heterogeneity and quantity? Existing research is lacking answers to such form of comparison.

Summarising the current state of knowledge, prediction markets are agreed to be the most effective way of aggregating dispersed knowledge into accurate forecasts across various platforms, categories, contracts and methodologies in open and closed applications. The influence of incentives has been analysed in cross-platform comparison and found to be sensitive to different categories. Other studies found days-to-expiry and volumes to be significant drivers of forecasting performance. The role of quantities vs. qualities has not yet been analysed extensively – leaving the question of whether a higher number of predictors results in higher forecasting performance or whether predictions by a small number of well-informed participants can predict as effectively.

3. Data

3.1 Data Provider

Data was derived through Matt Burgess, the CEO of iPredict (http://www.ipredict.co.nz). This dataset has not been studied in previous works and thus allows new insights into what factors accuracy depends upon.

iPredict began development in 2007 and launched to the public in September 2008, two months before the last New Zealand election. iPredict is owned by the University of Victoria and is acknowledged by the New Zealand Securities Commission. Today iPredict has over 3,300 registered users who have completed 426,000 trades of 11.7 million futures contracts worth $4.2 million.

Concerning technological development, ipredict is one of the world's most advanced prediction markets, offering several features that competing real-money markets are still missing. Most importantly, ipredict was the first real-money market to implement a modified form[2] of Hanson's market maker based on a logarithmic scoring rule (Hanson, 2002; 2003) for all traded contracts.

With few exceptions, other prediction markets (particularly real-money ones) apply continuous double auctions in which trading activity occurs when user-generated offers to buy or sell a stock at a defined price (optionally limited to a certain time range over which the offer is active) match in the order book.

Traders can choose between picking orders that already exist in the order book or set new prices which are contingent until matched by counterparty.

The major drawbacks of this trading mechanism are a lack in liquidity corresponding to substantial bid/ask spreads. This leads to a high numbers of unmatched offers and averts individual beliefs from influencing the current market price.

iPredict, on the contrary, subsidises liquidity and improves order clearing by operating an automated market maker based on Hanson's findings.

The market maker operates in real-money and play-money markets as a virtual trader. The purpose of this is to increase the number of matched orders without introducing bias, thus improving accuracy. The market maker continually makes offers to buy and sell according to a price schedule and seeding rules that are specified prior to the

---

[2] Ipredict.co.nz operates a non-continuous version of Hanson (2003;2003) logarithmic scoring rule

stock launch. This provides more accurate forecasts since information aggregation does not suffer from unmatched buy/sell orders.

Further, it is not sensitive to the number of traders active in the market. On the other hand, running this form of market maker exposes the operators to the risk of exposing proprietary funds and requires careful value-at-risk management to avoid arbitrary exploitation of market maker settings and monetary losses. The issue in running an automated market maker is its lack of sensitivity to new information, which is available to all human traders who process new information into an adjustment of individual beliefs.

Hence, market maker specifications are to be chosen carefully so that forecast accuracy does not suffer from individuals exploiting the market maker's inability to adjust prices with reference to new information. To cope with these issues, ipredict's market maker operates according to three settings decided at the time a new stock is established. The settings are:

Start Price: The initial market price which defines the price at which buy orders end and sell orders begin (default: 0.5).

Batch Size: The number of stocks offered at each price point.

Market Maker Sensitivity: All offers are made on an S-curve; the Sensitivity variable decides the steepness of this curve. The MM maker sets prices for all buy and sell offers using an S-curve. The formula for this S-curve is shown in [11].

Budget: Maximum loss during the lifetime of a contract. After the budget is exhausted, the MM quits operations on the side (buy/sell) that would put further value at risk.

For newly created contracts, the market maker calculates a price schedule according to equation [11]. Beginning from i=0, i increases in steps of 1 and computes a price for each marginal increase. Until this price is within 0.0001 of 0 computed prices are stored in arrays. Subsequently, this procedure is repeated for i decreasing in steps of 1. All buy/sell offers of the market maker are set according to the derived price schedule. 75% of all trades involved market maker activity as a buying/selling entity, the remainder was settled between two human traders.

$$[11] \quad Price_i = \frac{1}{1 + e^{\frac{i}{sensitivity}}}$$

where

i is]–n; n[

n is defined by the value that produces a price within 0.0001 of 0 or 1, the minimum and maximum prices (which depends on the Sensitivity setting). The system requires the sensitivity value to be in the range 0–99.

The market maker was operated in an identical manner for real- and play-money contracts.

Real-money trades (681,347 observations) occurred on iPredict's publicly available online market between 12.06.2008 13:59 and 06.03.2010 09:39. The dataset includes any trading observation within this time range. The license issued by the New Zealand Securities Commission imposes a number of restrictions on real-money event categories and user deposit amounts.

Contract variety is limited to political and economic contracts. Economic contracts are based on future interest rates, petrol prices and Official Cash Rate announcements; political contracts relate to elections, legislation and political scandals.

User deposits are limited to $500 per 6 calendar months. Gains in wealth (Y) from trading activity can exceed this limit with the current top trader holding a net worth of $7,600. Considering that iPredict has been operating for 2 years, a maximum amount of $2000 could have been deposited. Table 2 indicates a list of users' net worth.

Play money data (22,914 trades) was derived from a market named "prophet" exclusively open to second/third-year finance students at the University of Wellington between March and May 2009. Users were endowed with an initial stake of 1000 credits; the best-performing ones received $30 at the end of the experiment. Since there is no limitation in the scope of contracts, play-money contracts were more diverse than real-money ones and were not limited to political/economic contracts. Although some economic contracts were available, the majority of contracts were not similar to those traded on real-money markets and therefore excluded from analysis. Hence, out of the 624 real-money contracts and 21 play-money contracts that have been traded on iPredict since launch 18 relevant contracts (14 real-money, 4 play-money) were selected for analysis(N=44,169). Table 3 lists selected contracts with relevant attributes for analysis. Additional specifications of the event are shown in Table 4. 39,314 observations involved real-money contracts, 4,855 were based on play-money.

Each data point included the following attributes: date/hour/min/sec of trade, volume (denoted in NZ $), price, seller ID, buyer ID, contract type (binary/index).

Forecast error (FE), days-to-expiry (D) and aggregated volumes were also analysed.

3.2   Definition of Variables

Forecast Error (FE)

The forecast error (FE) constitutes the most significant variable for the further empirical analysis. For a wide range of empirical studies it has been applied as an estimator of the accuracy of predictions through measuring the spread between π_1 and expiry value (Wolfers & Zitzwitz, 2004). Per definition, FE equals 0 at expiry; as the true outcome is observed. By calculating the error term of the estimated probability it is valid to extract information on the quality of prediction at any given date for any given contract. In order for prediction markets to generate accurate forecasts at each point the FE is optimally low or zero.

[12] $\quad FE_{D,i} = \sqrt{(\pi_{D,i} - \pi_{D=0,i})^2}$

where

i = all, market, category, contract,

D = days-to-expiry

The average forecast error (AFE) equals the mean of all traded prices at point t. AFE allows for cross-contract comparison at different days-to-expiry without risking to pick a non-representative (high spread to AFE over the period) FE at a single trading point. It was computed for certain intervals prior to expiry (10-day intervals) as well as over the entire contract lifetime.

[13] $\quad AFE_{D,i} = \dfrac{\sum_{D=market\ launch}^{D=t} \sqrt{(\pi_{D,i} - \pi_{D=0,i})^2}}{N}$

Days-to-expiry (D)

Days-to-expiry (D) denotes the length of time between expiry date and the date at which trading activity occurred (t). For each trading activity D was computed. It was set as the first independent variable for regression on FEs to measure influence on information availability to market participants. The closer a contract gets to expiry the more information about the relevant event/index is available to the market participants. It is assumed that additional information pushes π_1 closer to the final value and thus reduces the average forecast error. Whether this assumption holds and if this also implies a reduction in volatility of traded prices will show in the further scope of analysis. Since the expiry date was set to the point where the market maker pays off to contract holders, D equals 0 for the last observed trading point in all contracts:

[13] $\quad D = (dd.mm.yyyy\ hh:mm)_{t=expiry} - (dd.mm.yyyy\ hh:mm)_t$

The Servan-Schreiber et al. (2004) study took trading prices that occurred prior to the relevant sports match. Since the payoff was determined after the sporting events, FE did not converge or equal zero for last trading activity; uncertainty remained high as the underlying sports event had not taken place at the point of last trading.

On iPredict, trading activity is possible until the MM pays off contracts held by traders (which occurs whenever the true outcome of an event is known). Hence the spread between the final trading price and expiry diminishes as D decreases. Specifically, the relationship between D and FE is expected to be non-linear as for some events uncertainty remains high despite low D. This observation can be explained by diverse degrees of heterogeneity in beliefs. For instance, a contract on a publicly traded industry index five minutes prior to market closing bears less uncertainty than a contract on whether interest rates will be lowered five minutes prior to the official press conference in which the decision will be announced. Clearly, the latter carries a higher degree of uncertainty. D was measured for each trading activity. To exclude D as influencing factor for measuring the influence of other parameters on different contracts, intervals were constructed for 10-day intervals of D.

Aggregated volume (AV)

Aggregated volume (AV) is the accumulated amount of discrete order volumes that have been traded until point t.

[14] $\quad AV = \sum_{D=0}^{D} \$\, amount\_traded_{D,i}$

An increase in AV can either be related to the quantity of trades or the quality of traded beliefs. Therefore, average order volumes (V) were computed to differentiate between quality and quantity. It is assumed that both types positively influence forecast accuracy and therefore yield negative influence on FE. AV was computed for any trading point, including the final trading point revealing the overall traded volume over contract lifetime, and set as second independent variable in the regression model

4. Results

4.1 Overall Data

Trading activity started 203 days prior to expiry, trading volumes are in the range [1–1502] and forecast errors lie between .0 (market maker activity was also included as a trading observation) and .62. Over the entire dataset, forecasts are fairly accurate, with a 81.83% mean accuracy. Table 5 contains a summary of descriptive statistics for the relevant variables.

Fifty per cent of trades involve less than $20, occured earlier than 21 days prior to expiry and yield forecast errors lower than 21%.

This high density of accurate, low-risk[3] trades is illustrated in Figures 2, 3 and 4. FEs show significant skewness (-.223 from the mean of 0.18) with a high density of trades at low FEs, or high accuracy, respectively.

From Figures 2 and 3 it can be inferred that the underlying cause for this observation is the substantial number of trades close to expiry (low D) with small trading volumes (V) at which market prices have approached expiry value and thus allow for marginal low-risk gains from risk-adverse trading activity. This finding supports the theoretical model discussed in earlier sections according to which higher demand/supply is expected for π_1 / π_0 being close to expiry values, which generally occurs shortly prior to expiry. The underlying hypotheses of risk-averse trading behaviour (logarithmic utility functions) proved to hold in the empirical data. The majority of trading amounts involved low volumes at high levels of information availability and low D.

Maximum trading volumes (V) of $1,000 (real-money) and $1,500 (play-money) allow for the interpretation that less risk-averse rationales are also present. Considering the fact that changes in wealth endowment were limited under both incentive schemes ($500 per 6 months for real-money; $1,000 for play-money), trading volumes of such scale involve a large share of overall trading funds placed on a single event. Rationales behind such trading activity can either be related to higher risk-tolerance for identical information signals or insider knowledge ("better"

---

[3] The low volumes of trading activity are interpreted as estimators for low risk-tolerance and the acsence of private information.

information set), which lowers risk-exposure as private information about the event is held by a limited number of traders.

4.2 Real-Money vs. Play-Money: Portfolio Comparison

Comparison of all selected contracts (Table 6) reveals that play-money yields lower average forecast errors (play-money mean FE 13.9% vs. real-money mean 18.7%).

Notably, both types differed not only in the number of observed trades but also in terms of underlying events that were traded.

Both incentive types generate equally good forecasts (play money: 6.9% vs. real money: 6.1%) within a 5% percentile.

This marginal spread widens above the 25th percentile and shows a substantial diversity at the 50th percentile: Play-money markets generate 9.7% average FE, real-money markets are less than half as accurate (22.56%). For clustered D (10-day intervals) play-money market average forecast errors within the intervals acknowledg this finding. For all intervals except D=[-45;-35] real-money contracts were less accurate (Table 10) yet this spread is lacking statistical significance (p-value: 0.11).

Average trading volumes (V) are nearly 4 times higher for play-money markets ($91 vs. $22). 5% of real-money trades involved trades of less than $1, whereas play-money contracts involved $15 at the same percentile.

Independent from the underlying events that were traded, play-money proved to be more accurate and generated higher trading volumes. Direct contract comparison will identify if this is caused by contract heterogeneity or systematic factors.

The positive influence of order volumes (= number of contracts) found across all trading activity requires further discussion: Firstly, users begin trading with equal trading funds under play-money markets, however, vary in initial endowment under real-money settings. Second, changes in Y can be caused/not caused by compensating for shrinking value through depositing external capital in real-money markets/play-money markets.

Under real-money circumstances users hold uneven trading balances. Therefore, high-volume trades are not necessarily motivated by excess knowledge but can in fact be "bad" trades by users with large amounts of externally deposited wealth endowments (as opposed to wealth enhancement resulting from "good" predicting). As maximum deposit amounts are capped on iPredict such irrationality has no substantial influence on market prices. Such irrationality has two-fold effects: Firstly, market prices reflect untruthfully revealed subjective beliefs if traders engage in irrational trading. Second, negative externalities can occur if the market-maker runs out of funds as a direct result of massive market-price movement through irrational trading. Both effects are mitigated by the cap in trading funds (for real- and play-money). Large-scale trading volumes bear the potential to violate this assumption under low states of overall liquidity if a market maker similar to that of iPredict is operating. A hypothetical case of unlimited user deposits and a market maker similar to that of ipredict would cause the market maker to stop operating once the threshold of maximum losses is reached. Under continuous double auctions high-order volumes are only partially cleared, as a lack of an equally sized counter-position results in the majority of stock offers being unmatched.

In play-money markets users are rewarded for revealing information through market trades by a winner's price (usually through prices or a small amount of money).

In the dataset underlying this paper the winner(s) received $30 at the end of the experiment. The winner is defined as the individual who holds the highest amount of trading funds at the end of the experiment. Since trading funds only change through previous trading gains/losses, only users with a track record of accurate predictions have the ability to place high-volumes. This limitation is not present in real-money markets and ensures that high-volume orders, which influence the market price more severely, can only be placed by individuals who have shown a history of accurate predictions.

Aggregated trading volumes over contract lifetime (Table 7) range from $4,447 to $291,723. The overall average is $74,229 for all contracts. Real money contracts on average attracted $74,229 or $52,049 when excluding the two large contracts on the NZ 2008 that generated massively higher volume than any other contract. Play-money contracts exceed this figure by 115% for contracts excluding those based on the 2008 election, and 48% for all analysed stocks.

In summary these findings reveal that play-money markets achieve higher quality in predictions (high order volumes limited to users with "good" track record) whereas real-money markets, on average, generate higher quantities (estimated by AV divided by V). Quantity, defined as the number of traders willing to participate in trading a particular contract, makes market efficient has positive effect on forecasting accuracy through mean regression.

Market efficiency is a necessary condition for accurate forecast generation. Fama (1970) defines markets as efficient if all available information (public and private) is reflected in the corresponding market price. Efficient markets "fully reflect all available information" (Fama, 1970, p. 383). In order to process new information efficiently, sufficient trading volumes/liquidity are necessary. Therefore, quantity is assumed to be a necessary condition for prediction markets to be efficient. Smith (1982), on the other hand, found that a relatively small number of individuals exposed to private information signals are sufficient for market efficiency.

Mean regression refers to a high number of uninformed contributors being capable of generating accurate estimations independently of expert knowledge. The example described in the introduction showed how unskilled participants generated a surprisingly accurate mean. Even if some or all individuals estimate at low accuracy, a large number of submissions can yield an accurate mean based upon high inaccuracy above/below the actual mean. In this sense, quantity can be seen as one reason for the accuracy of large crowds.

For instance the audience in *Who Wants to be a Millionaire* generates accurate answers 92% of the time, whereas chosen experts knew the right answer only 65% of the time Surowiecki (2004).

Quality in predictions refers to individuals trading private signals that are not available as public information. Public information is available to all individuals (e.g. press releases, online news agencies, blogs, newspapers, etc.). Public information can be directly or indirectly related to the specific event. Referring to the hypothetical example from the introduction, information on Iran's GDP might indirectly influence stock prices whereas the discovery of unknown testing facilities for nuclear missiles has a more direct influence on the occurrence of the event and therefore yields a higher momentum on the stock price. Trading activity continues until the new market-price reflects all available knowledge. The availability of information is highly specific to single contracts and cannot be generalized across categories.

Private information is defined as information sets that are held by a limited number of traders (also referred to as "insider knowledge"). Any individual in possession of private information has more accurate information than is reflected in the market price. This yields potential for unsystematic excess return under semi-strong markets. Rational traders in possession of such information leverage excess returns by placing high order volumes. From this perspective, it is valid to relate high trading volumes to private information for real-money trading. Whether traders are willing to reveal private information under play-money markets is questionable. However, since high order-volumes imply previous accuracy in trading the causality between volumes and quality holds as well, although the underlying concept is a different one.

In summary, under both money types, order volumes can be interpreted as estimator for the quality of contributed trade.

Therefore, the quality-related excess accuracy of play-money contracts can be interpreted in four ways:

1.) Under real-money settings traders with bad predictions have the possibility to compensate for losses in Y by depositing external money. The inability to do so under play-money contracts provides strong incentives to avoid losses through trading activity as running out of funds excludes individuals from further trading. Additionally, high volume trades are not possible for "bad" traders. Hypothetically, a similar correlation between volumes and quality exists under real-money contracts; however, users with bad predictions are not excluded from trading. Play-money contracts therefore predict better as a result of excluding unsuccessful traders and allowing major changes in market-prices only through traders who have predicted accurately previously.

2.) Selection of traders influences quality. The play-money market was limited to finance students; the real-money market, on the other hand does not make any limitation as to who is involved in trading. Presumably, some traders in the open real-money market contribute lower quality than finance students for various reasons (cognitive, amout of reflected information, etc.). The finding of similarly accurate predictions in the 1st percentile argues in favour of this hypothesis, as a small number of trades in the real-money market were "just as good" as under play-money. At the 50th percentile the spread in quality becomes more obvious as quality is constant under play-money whereas real-money accuracy suffers from worse predictions.

3.) Influencing activity: Prediction markets can be instrumentalized in the form of manipulating the outcome of an event or by influencing market-prices to deliberately create false predictions. Sport betting has illustrated the consequences of individuals unlawfully influencing the outcome of events in order to maximize financial payoffs. Current prediction markets lack the scale and liquidity to show such reciprocity, especially when making limitations to user deposits.

Influencing activity, on the contrary, has been observed in prediction market trading: The election campaign team around George Bush short-sold stock in the 2004 election (Rothschild & Wolfers, 2008) in order to encourage undecided voters to vote for Bush. Such influencing activity is less likely to occur under play-money settings as multiple accounts would have to be opened and media reporting on prediction market forecasts usually involves real-money markets.

4.) Contract-specificity: Spreads in mean forecast errors are sensitive to underlying events. Whether this interpretation holds will show in the following direct contract comparison.

4.3 Real-Money vs. Play-Money: Direct Contract Comparison

Four contracts with equal event categories (currency exchange rates), payoff structure (indexed) and market design (market maker) were chosen. By picking contracts with equal parameters, except for different incentives schemes (play-money/real-money) and the number of active traders (real money = open market; play money = closed market), deviations can be attributed to the variables assumed to influence forecasting performance.

In order to analyse event specificity, three contracts (one play-money, two real-money) were chosen to be perfectly identical ("What will the NZ dollar be worth against the AUZ dollar") and one play-money contract was picked on a slightly different event ("What will the NZ dollar be worth against the EUR")?

Tables 8 (play-money contracts) and 9 (real-money contracts) show that real-money contracts exhibit marginally better average forecasting performance with means of 5.0% (contract ID 82) and 3% (contract ID 84) compared to play-money incentives (6.6% for contract ID 35) based on events on the exchange rate between NZ /AUZ $.

The contract on the EUR/NZ exchange rate, on the contrary, demonstrates substantially lower accuracy over the entire contract lifetime (mean: 21%).

The fact that the mean of these contracts is far more accurate than the mean of the overall dataset can be explained by the payoff structure (indexed vs. binary). Table 16 showed that identical contracts (NZ 2008 election) with different payoff structures (binary vs. indexed) yielded significant spreads in aggregated forecast mean. This finding also holds on a general level and shows statistical significance at all conficence levels (t-stat: 7.37). The accuracy of real-money contracts shows a negative relationship to the number of trading observations. Real-money contracts attract much fewer trades (contract ID 82: 262; contract ID 84: 408, contract ID35: 1,664) but nevertheless generat highly accurate forecasts with a maximum inaccuracy of 10.88%. Notably, this spread is present over all percentiles. Order volumes do not differ in terms of average money traded, although contract 37 (EUR/NZ) shows a remarkably high maximum trading volume. An order volume of $1,502 is nearly three times as large as the highest-volume trade in contract ID 35 and 15 times higher than the maximum volumes in real-money contract 82 (7 times as high as real-money contract 84).

Table 10 shows the comparison of AFE within 10-day intervals. The higher real-money accuracy is present over all intervals and statistically significant (t-stat: -6.9), showing that real-money demonstrate that information aggregation is more accurate under real-money when holding all other factors constant. The significant spread (t-value: -15.0) among play-money AFE intervals further shows high event-specific heterogeneity (contract ID 35 vs. contract ID 37).

This heterogeneity can either be related to external factors (information availability) or unobservable trading dynamics.

For both play-money contracts the volatility in currency exchange rates was analysed over the contract lifetimes. Potentially, subjective beliefs on the NZ/EUR exchange rate suffer from a higher inaccuracy owing to a lower ascendancy compared to the NZ/AUZ rate. The root of variance in the NZ/AUZ exchange rate equals 0.015 while the NZ/EUR exchange rate variance was lower (0.007). Hence, more subtle factors must have caused this spread, which cannot be detected by quantitative analysis.

The results show that play-money generates slightly better predictions than play-money in direct comparison. Indexed contracts are more accurate than binary ones and most importantly, trading dynamics are highly sensitive to underlying events and cannot be generalized.

4.4 Real-Money/Play-Money: Influencing Factors

Since play-money markets were open for a limited period of time, trades occurred later than in real-money markets (min d_play: -48.8 vs. min d_real: 203.9).Taking the entire dataset into account, even 80 days prior to the event, average forecast errors (AFE) are substantially lower (14.5%) than in the Servan-Schreiber et al. (2004) study where final trading prices prior to sports events were measured (d<0). Assuming market efficiency in both platforms, this reveals a lower level of absolute uncertainty on iPredict contracts. Without direct comparison, however, it is not clear what role deposit limits, market maker settings, and other systematic factors play in explaining this excess accuracy. On ipredict uncertainty does not decrease significantly as contracts move towards expiry.

The mean AFE decreases from 14.5% 80 days prior to expiry to 8.9% 40 days before. After this point, AFE does not pursue this trend but becomes less accurate and more volatile. There are various explanations for this observation. Either users entering in this late phase contribute beliefs of less accuracy than those of "early" predictors, or the same traders who have traded before make less accurate predictions. For either explanation a higher number of trades do not yield more accurate predictions.

A direct comparison on all equal, or similar, contracts (IDs 35, 37, 82 & 84 referring to pay offs on the NZ/AUZ exchange rate, ID 37 on the NZ/EUR exchange rate) in clustered intervals, shows that aggregated FEs do not follow a linear downward slope, but exhibit side-movements or even upward-movements as contracts approach expiry. Other contracts, however, are shown to be in line with the hypotheses of additional public information, with lower Ds related to increased forecast accuracy.

Uncertainty does not decrease in a linear manner.

For D not being clustered into intervals, Figures 7 and 8 imply a general negative relationship for late contract phases. This non-linear relationship starts earlier under real-money: contract ID 82 follows a downward-trend starting 35 days prior to expiry, the average forecast error of contract ID 84 declines 60 days before at a higher degree of side-movement. Play-money trades, on the contrary, do not show such dynamics until D<5. The decline is much more massive and causes forecast errors to drop from high inaccuracy-levels towards FE approaching zero within short time ranges. This effect is more severe for contract ID 35 whereas contract ID 37 does not show any dependence on days to expiry at higher absolute accuracy.

Figures 9 and 10 further illustrate the low sensitivity of FE to aggregated trading volumes. Whereas real-money contracts show some dependency, such dependency is not observable for play-money contracts (Table 6). The statistical models built to verify the influence of D and AV (table 12 and 13) support the hypotheses of positive influence by decreasing D and increasing AV on forecasting accuracy.

However, R^2 of .13 for play-money contracts (IDs 35 & 39) and .25 for real-money (IDs 82 & 84) indicate that this effect is far less intense than expected. Again, two explanations are possible to explain this result: Either there is no significant and systematic relationship between the analysed parameters or contracts show high degrees of heterogeneity leading to low overall sensitivity. Since forecasting accuracy was found to be contract-specific it is most likely that influencing factors show the same degree of heterogeneity across traded events. Additional research is required to discuss this matter further.

4.5. Conclusion

This paper has analysed 44,179 trading observations from iPredict.co.nz under real-money and play-money incentives.

Inferred insights from this paper were based on markets subsidized by a market-maker. Hence, findings cannot be inferred as generic knowledge on markets operating a continuous double auction and cannot be compared directly to previous studies on different datasets. It was found that theoretical frameworks developed by previous studies hold for this study's trading observations. Accuracy was found to depend on incentives, specific contracts and volumes.

Play-money incentives generated more accurate results on a portfolio consisting of different events. In direct contract comparison, however, real-money was proven to be the more effective incentive scheme. This finding reveals two relevant insights. First, real-money predicts better when holding all other parameters constant. Second, trading dynamics are highly sensitive to the underlying event and contract-specific trading dynamics.

A negative correlation between the number of order volumes and accuracy was found in a comparison of all trading observations and in direct contract comparison.

A low number of high-volume trading occurrences were more accurate than a high number of risk-averse trades involving low volumes at market prices already close to expiry value. A hypothesis to be tested by further research should address the question whether order volume (# of contracts) in fact depends on the quality of information and under which circumstances this effect holds.

The presumed influence of days-to-expiry was weaker and less significant than expected. Whether the lower sensitivity to newly available information is caused by uneven distribution of relevant information, market inefficiency or other factors, remains an open issue for further research.

Do some crowds predict better than others? Empirical findings suggest they do: Real-money incentives and higher average order amounts positively influence forecasting accuracy for equal events. In this sense, doubling the ticket prices for the ox wager presumably would have predicted the weight 100% accurate.

References

Arrow, K., Forsythe, R., Gorham, M., Hahn, R., Hanson, R., Ledyard, J., et al. (2008). The Promise of Prediction Markets. *Science 16.* pp. 877-878.

Berg, J., Forsythe, R., & Rietz, T. (1996). What Makes Markets Predict Well? Evidence from the IOWA Electronic Markets. In W. G. W Albers, *Understanding Strategic Interaction: Essay in Honor of Reinhard Selten* (pp. 444-463). New York: Springer.

Berg, J. E., R. Forsythe, F. D., Nelson, & T. A. Rietz .(2008a). Results from a Dozen Years of Election Futures Markets Research. In: C. R. Plott und V. L. Smith (ed.): The Handbook of Experimental Economics Results, Volume 1, pp. 742-751. North Holland.

Berg, J. E., Nelson, F. D., & Rietz, T. A. (2008a). Prediction Market Accuracy in the Long Run. *International Journal of Forecasting. 24 (2)* pp. 285-295.

Chen, K.-Y., & Plott, C. (2002). Information Aggregation Mechanisms: Concept, Design and Implementation for a Sales Forecasting Problem. *California Institute of Technology Social Science Working Paper No. 1131.*

Cowgill, B., Wolfers, J., & Zitzewitz, E. (2008). *Using Prediction Markets to Track Information Flows: Evidence from Google.* Derived from www.bocowgill.com/GooglePredictionMarketPaper.pdf (accessed 1 August 2010)

Fama, E. F, 1970. Efficient Capital Markets: A Review of Theory and Empirical Work," Journal of Finance, American Finance Association. 25(2) pp. 383-417.

Forsythe, R., Rietz, T., & Ross, T. (1999). Wishes, Expectations and Actions: A Survey on Price Formation in Election Stock Markets. *Journal of Economic Behavior & Organization.* 39 pp. 83–110.

Grossman, J., S., & Stiglitz, J. E. (1976). Information and Competetive Price Systems. *The American Economic Review.* 66 (2) pp. 246-253.

Hanson, R. (2002). Logarithmic Market Scoring Rules for Modular Combinatorial Information Aggregation. Derived from http://hanson.gmu.edu/mktscore.pdf (accessed 1 August 2010)

Hanson, R. (2003). Combinatorial Information Market Design. *Information Systems Frontiers.* 5(1) pp. 107-119.

Hayek, F. A. (1945). The Use of Knowledge in Society. *The American Review.* 35 (4) pp. 519-530

Ivanow, A. (2009). Using Prediction Markets to Harness Collective Wisdom for Forecasting. *The Journal of Business Forecasting*, 28 (3) pp. 9-14.

Jacobs, V. (2009). *Prediction Markets: How They Work and how Well They Work.* Master thesis, Katholieke Universiteit, Leuven.

Kahneman, D., & Tversky, A. (1979). Prospect Theory: An Analysis of Decision under Risk. *Econometrica.* 47 (2) pp. 263-292.

Looney, R. (2003). DARPA's Policy Analysis Market for Intelligence: Outside the Box or Off the Wall. *Strategic Insights, September, 2:9.*

Luckner, S. (2008). Prediction Markets: Fundamentals, Key Design Elements, and Applications. *The 21st Bled eConference, eCollaboration: Overcoming Boundaries Through Multi-Channel Interaction.* Bled, Slovenia.

Manski, C. (2004). Interpreting the Predictions of Prediction Markets. *NBER Working Paper 10359.* March 2004.

Pennock, D., Larence, S., Nielsen, F., & Giles, C. (2001). The Real Power of Artifical Markets. *Science.* 291 (5506) pp. 987-988.

Polk, C., Hanson, R., Ledyard, J. , & Ishikida, T. (2003). Policy Analysis Market: An Electronic Commerce Application of a Combinatorial Information Market. In *Proceedings of the Fourth ACM Conference on Electronic Commerce*, 272–3.

Rosenbloom, E., & Notz, W. (2006). Statistical Tests of Real-Money Versus Play-Money Prediction Markets. *Eletronic Markets.* 16 (1) pp. 63-69.

Rothschild, D., & Wolfers, J. (2008). Market Manipulation Muddies Election Outlook. Derived from http://online.wsj.com/article/SB122283114935193363.html. (accessed 1 August 2010)

Servan-Schreiber, E., Wolfers, J., Pennock, D., & Galebach, B. (2004). Prediction Markets: Does Money Matter? *Electronic Markets.* 14 (3) pp. 243-251.

Smith, V. L. (1982). Markets as Economizer of Information: Experimental Examination of the Hayek-Hypothesis. *Economic Inquiry.* 20 pp. 165-179.

Spann, M., & Skiera, B. (2009). Sports Forecasting: A Comparison of the Forecast Accuracy of Prediction Markets, Betting Odds and Tipsters. *Journal of Forecasting.* 28 (1) pp. 55-72.

Surowiecki, James (2004). *The Wisdom of Crowds: Why the Many Are Smarter Than the Few and How Collective Wisdom Shapes Business, Economies, Societies and Nations*, Doubleday, New York.

Tziralis, G.,& Tatsiopoulos, I. (2007), Prediction Markets: An Extended Literature Review, *Journal of Prediction Markets.* 1(1) pp. 75-91.

Wolfers, J., & Zitzewitz, E. (2004). Prediction Markets. *Journal of Economic Perspectives*. 18 (2) pp. 107-126.

Wolfers, J., & Zitzewitz, E. (2006a). Interpreting Prediction Market Prices as Probabilities. *Discussion Paper Series IZA DP No. 2092*.

Wolfers, J., & Zitzewitz, E. (2006b). Prediction Markets in Theory and Practice. *Discussion Paper Series IZA DP No. 1991*.

Appendix

Market Name	Iowa Electronic Markets	Intrade	Betfair	Bet2Give	NewsFutures	Hubdub	Foresight Exchange	Inkling Markets
Internet Address	www.biz.uiowa.edu/iem/	www.intrade.com	www.betfair.com	www.bet2give.com	us.newsfutures.com	www.hubdub.com	www.ideosphere.com	home.inklingmarkets.com
Founded	1988	2001	2000	2007	2000	2008	1994	2006
Real Money?	Yes	Yes	Yes	Yes (all trading profits are given to charity)	No ("eXchange dollars")	No ("Hubdub dollars")	No ("FX-bucks")	No
Purpose of the market	Research	Financial market	Betting exchange	Encourage charitable donations	Entertainment	Entertainment	Entertainment	Entertainment
Incentives to trade	Financial gain	Financial gain	Financial gain	leaderboard, donations list, giving to charity	leaderboards, social networking features, play-money can be used in auctions for real prizes	leaderboards, player levels, social networking features	leaderboards	leaderboards, social networking features
How are contracts issued?	traders can buy unit portfolios from the market	matching of buyers and sellers in order book	a back bet is matched with a lay bet in the order book	matching of buyers and sellers in order book	each contract has an opposite; matching of buyers of one contract with buyers of its opposite contract	market scoring rule acts as market maker	matching of buyers and sellers in order book	market scoring rule acts as market maker
Trading mechanism	continuous double auction	continuous double auction	continuous double auction	continuous double auction	continuous double auction	Hanson's market scoring rule	continuous double auction	Hanson's market scoring rule
Information available to traders	current prices, last prices, historical data	complete order book, historical data	complete order book	complete order book, names of traders, historical data	complete order book, names of traders, historical data	current probabilities, prediction history, names of traders	complete order book, names of traders, historical data	current probabilities, prediction history, names of traders
Contract price range	$0 to $1	$0 to $10 (0 to 100 points)	decimal odds	$0 to $1	X$0 to X$100	0% to 100%	0 FX-cent to 100 FX-cent	$0 to $100
Min/Max investment	min $5, max $500	min $25, max -	min £5, max -	min $5, max $300	receive X$2,000 at registration, no maximum	receive H$1,000 at registration, no maximum	receive $FX2,900 at registration, no maximum	receive $5,000 (play-money) at registration, no maximum
Fees	activation charge ($5), no trading fees	variable per trade + expiry fee	commission on winnings	None	None	None	None	None
2008 U.S. presidential election contracts	WTA Democrat, WTA Republican, VS Democrat VS Republican	WTA Democrat, WTA Republican, WTA Obama, WTA McCain	WTA Obama, WTA McCain	WTA Democrat	WTA Democrat	WTA Obama, WTA McCain	WTA Democrat	WTA Obama

$ = U.S. dollar, £ = Pound sterling, WTA = winner-take-all, VS = vote-share

Table 1 (Jacobs, 2009, p. 10) Overview of various online prediction markets with relevant design characteristics

Total Traders: 3308

Ranked by Net Worth. Click here to rank by Return On Investment

#	Trading Name	Amount (Change)		#	Trading Name	Amount (Change)	
1	dpf	($0.34 ↓)	$7,588.22	51	ABCD1234	($10.85 ↓)	$1,062.79
2	ST00	($151.90 ↑)	$6,476.28	52	XYZ123	($536.92 ↑)	$1,044.88
3	Hunn	($7.99 ↑)	$6,119.38	53	Elum	($415.60 ↑)	$1,036.64
4	Legs	($263.09 ↓)	$5,435.46	54	stickybun	($2.81 ↓)	$1,010.83
5	Ditoo	($54.73 ↓)	$5,379.49	55	izzy	(NC)	$1,010.39
6	Brew	($13.05 ↓)	$5,323.96	56	sativa	(NC)	$1,000.00
7	tekurafarm	($34.76 ↑)	$4,587.35	57	MikesRetirementFund	($3.34 ↑)	$977.61
8	neno	($1.29 ↓)	$4,445.86	58	Zirons	($17.21 ↑)	$973.20
9	ECrampton	($191.30 ↓)	$4,425.19	59	scottyc007	($380.63 ↑)	$972.45
10	Caml	($8.98 ↓)	$3,387.18	60	Ikeng	(NC)	$947.91
11	dray	($5.59 ↑)	$3,088.12	61	felix	(NC)	$928.96
12	defaultswap	($159.12 ↑)	$2,734.49	62	melonista	(NC)	$911.85
13	Sejanus	($0.16 ↓)	$2,716.91	63	landslide	($285.85 ↓)	$900.72
14	hion	($5.19 ↑)	$2,648.68	64	pipe42	($2.28 ↑)	$890.83
15	BossHog	($3.04 ↑)	$2,634.22	65	walkdontrun	(NC)	$882.58
16	rene_lp	($1.75 ↑)	$2,467.94	66	buxio122	($0.98 ↑)	$874.40
17	Stirtrader	($1.10 ↑)	$2,456.77	67	Vici	($28.70 ↑)	$836.70
18	KentStevens	($79.49 ↑)	$2,425.00	68	Predictable	($330.03 ↑)	$834.23
19	corbusian	($260.41 ↓)	$2,416.10	69	polaris	($13.97 ↑)	$795.71
20	Funfinite	($1.97 ↓)	$2,370.29	70	sparkyoraig	($3.12 ↑)	$791.65
21	RadiataPine	($107.45 ↑)	$2,369.99	71	nikzang	($3.14 ↑)	$739.88
22	Willnz	($0.29 ↑)	$2,252.74	72	JoshuaJ	($2.77 ↑)	$732.21
23	Create	($710.17 ↓)	$2,155.50	73	jonnyQuid	(NC)	$720.75
24	Taurusport	(NC)	$2,127.80	74	cassandra	($39.18 ↑)	$677.82
25	Eclipse	($318.60 ↑)	$2,007.68	75	callan	($15.02 ↑)	$669.26
26	Fidel	($4.95 ↑)	$1,959.98	76	liq374	($22.16 ↑)	$640.45
27	Economist	($12.15 ↑)	$1,926.91	77	Mumdad	($2.08 ↑)	$631.02
28	Shotover	(NC)	$1,924.73	78	Esteban	($7.00 ↑)	$619.92
29	Okanenichi	($55.64 ↑)	$1,740.11	79	sleemanj	($4.61 ↓)	$610.66
30	Zinicene	($107.57 ↑)	$1,661.89	80	plutoman	(NC)	$608.98
31	Smasher	($0.44 ↑)	$1,567.97	81	diadithinkigotitwrong...	($0.74 ↑)	$602.98
32	smartypants	($1.21 ↑)	$1,544.48	82	SouthCoast	(NC)	$580.45
33	Gloria	($15.80 ↑)	$1,475.35	83	GuessWho	($0.44 ↑)	$578.50
34	blackdog	($45.25 ↓)	$1,442.28	84	Razork	($1.51 ↓)	$572.17
35	HiDon	($0.63 ↑)	$1,373.99	85	Yesom	($1.52 ↑)	$544.35
36	mgaamoleyey	($1.40 ↑)	$1,373.23	86	best_betas	(NC)	$535.25
37	libero	($3.77 ↓)	$1,299.20	87	KeethDagilish	($4.35 ↑)	$529.89
38	Casey9	($7.67 ↑)	$1,296.52	88	hardthinker	($3.11 ↑)	$521.30
39	BroadArrow	($117.47 ↑)	$1,271.02	89	Quilx	($0.62 ↑)	$514.46
40	adamsmith	($14.90 ↑)	$1,246.49	90	shatec	($1.40 ↑)	$501.64
41	jmvm	($5.76 ↓)	$1,224.18	91	UCFamily	(NC)	$500.00
42	Sell	($389.89 ↑)	$1,210.12	92	Pablo	($23.54 ↑)	$494.19
43	Artist	($14.40 ↑)	$1,160.94	93	AAA!	($22.22 ↑)	$493.96
44	greyghost	($4.02 ↑)	$1,159.69	94	ohokavillager	($35.38 ↑)	$492.36
45	Ibid	($3.38 ↑)	$1,156.99	95	FATCAT	($54.18 ↑)	$484.02
46	Alan3285	($2.89 ↑)	$1,131.62	96	MrMag	($17.29 ↑)	$481.83
47	Trax	(NC)	$1,122.84	97	Covergirl86	($5.03 ↑)	$464.19
48	ELIQ	($9.44 ↑)	$1,111.08	98	Dude	($4.16 ↑)	$461.10
49	Arsenii	(NC)	$1,073.33	99	fredphillips	($7.61 ↑)	$456.19
50	ORACLE	($0.04 ↑)	$1,072.09	100	solutionpartner	(NC)	$452.12

Data displayed as at 15/08/2010 02:43:40

Table 2. (www.ipredict.co.nz): List of ipredict real-money traders sorted by net worth/available trading funds (Y)

ID	i= internal/external	i=political/ economic	i=binary/ indexed	i=play/ real money	contract
1-2	internal	political	binary	real	NZ election
4-5	internal	political	indexed	real	NZ election
21-22	external	political	binary	real	US election
35	external	cconomic	indexed	play	NZ $/ AU$
37	external	economic	indexed	play	NZ $ / EUR
39	external	economic	indexed	play	NZ $/ AU$
41	internal	exam	binary	play	Exam
69	internal	economic	binary	real	GDP negative
82	external	economic	indexed	real	NZ $ / US $
84	external	economic	indexed	real	NZ $ / US $
121-124	internal	economic	binary	real	ΔInterest rates
292	external	int. relations	binary	real	North Korea missile

Table 3. (Own illustration): List of all 18 analyzed contracts showing contract ID, relevant attributes, description

contract ID	description of event
1	There will be a Labour Prime Minister after the 2008 election
2	There will be a National Prime Minister after the 2008 election
4	What share of the party vote will Labour win at the 2008 election? (stock pays 1c/1% vote)
5	What share of the party vote will National win at the 2008 election? (stock pays 1c/1% vote)
21	Barack Obama to be elected US President in 2008 election
22	John McCain to be elected US President in 2008 election
35	NZ dollar/Australian dollar exchange rate at end of April
37	NZ dollar/Euro exchange rate at end of May
39	NZ dollar/Australian dollar exchange rate at end of May
41	MOFI 201 2nd test median 60% - 64%
69	GDP growth to be negative in September quarter
82	What will the New Zealand dollar be worth against the greenback in January 2009?
84	What will the New Zealand dollar be worth against the greenback in March 2009?
121	Reserve Bank of Australia to lower cash rate by 75 basis points on 3 February 2009
122	Reserve Bank of Australia to lower cash rate by 50 basis points on 3 February 2009
123	Reserve Bank of Australia to lower cash rate by 25 basis points on 3 February 2009
124	Reserve Bank of Australia to not lower cash rate by 25, 50, 75 or 100 basis points on 3 February 2009
292	North Korea to fire a missile at a foreign country in 2009

Table 4 (Own illustration): List of all 18 analysed contracts showing contract ID and event description.

stats	fe_all	v_all	d_all
mean	.1817402	30.25013	-27.298
min	0	0	-203.94
max	.6243	1502	0
sd	.1136145	37.58337	28.81194
p5	.0069	1	-63.07
p25	.0563	7	-40.87
p50	.2198	20	-21.22
N	44169	44169	44169

Table 5 (Own illustration): Descriptive statistics for forecast errors (FE), trading volumes (V) and days to expiry (D) for all observed trading occurrences.

stats	fe_real	fe_play	d_real	d_play	v_real	v_play
mean	.187014	.1390349	-27.06878	-29.15409	22.72936	91.15057
min	0	0	-203.94	-48.8	0	1
max	.6243	.5977	0	0	1000	1502
sd	.1107597	.1266864	29.99387	16.23289	24.37365	62.23857
p5	.0069	.0061	-63.29	-46.9	1	15
p25	.0718	.0334	-40.11	-43.5	6	91
p50	.2256	.0966	-20.14222	-35.4	17	100
N	39314	4855	39314	4855	39314	4855

Table 6 (Own illustration): Descriptive statistics for forecast errors (FE), trading volumes (V) and days to expiry (D) for real-money observations (real) and play money observations (play).

stats	fe_id35	fe_id37	d_id35	d_id37	v_id_35	v_id_37
mean	.0665103	.2142947	-25.26532	-27.78531	92.63582	94.18182
min	0	0	-48.3	-48.8	1	1
max	.4274	.4901	0	0	600	1502
sd	.0678733	.1246731	16.6128	17.29103	41.26997	74.04391
p5	.0061	.0167	-46.2	-47.4	26	15
p25	.0227	.1313	-42.9	-45.7	100	99
p50	.0443	.1922	-16.2	-33.5	100	100
N	1664	1892	1664	1892	1664	1892

Table 7 (Own illustration): List of analysed contracts showing contract ID, relevant attributes, and overall traded volumes (AV)

ID	AV	real/play money
1	$ 291,723	real
2	$ 252,471	real
4	$ 17,711	real
5	$ 16,592	real
21	$ 96,312	real
22	$ 115,140	real
35	$ 154,146	play
37	$ 178,192	play
39	$ 60,690	play
41	$ 49,508	play
69	$ 13,862	real
82	$ 4,447	real
84	$ 6,709	real
121	$ 20,788	real
122	$ 12,753	real
123	$ 11,687	real
124	$ 22,201	real
292	$ 11,186	real

Table 8 (Own illustration): Descriptive statistics for forecast errors (FE), trading volumes (V) and days to expiry (D) for play-money contracts on currency exchange rates.

stats	fe_id82	fe_id84	d_id82	d_id84	v_id_82	v_id_84
mean	.0498038	.0300613	−25.64517	−58.15875	17.03831	16.44363
min	0	0	−40.54	−102.98	0	1
max	.1088	.1008	0	0	100	200
sd	.025717	.0236601	12.81745	31.74931	13.83385	16.55226
p5	.0078	.0008	−40.47	−102.84	1	1
p25	.0225	.0159	−37.63	−90.47	8	5
p50	.0555	.01995	−28.62	−54.01	16	16.5
N	261	408	261	408	261	408

Table 9 (Own illustration): Descriptive statistics for forecast errors (FE), trading volumes (V) and days to expiry (D) for real-money contracts on currency exchange rates.

D_intervals	-80	-70	-60	-50	-40	-30	-20	-10
afe_all	14.5%	13.2%	12.9%	9.6%	8.9%	10.8%	14.0%	11.5%
afe_play				6.6%	10.1%	7.8%	12.2%	9.5%
afe_real	14.5%	13.2%	12.9%	11.2%	8.4%	12.0%	14.7%	12.3%

Table 10 (Own illustration): Comparison of forecast errors, days to expiry and trading volumes between real- and play-money markets.

D_intervals	-40	-30	-20	-10
afe_ID_35	5.9%	5.3%	5.6%	5.7%
Δ		-0.6%	0.3%	0.1%
afe_ID_37	25.5%	22.4%	21.6%	20.3%
Δ		-3.1%	-0.9%	-1.3%
afe_ID_39	16.9%	19.0%	20.7%	24.1%
Δ		2.1%	1.7%	3.3%
afe_ID_82	5.1%	6.5%	5.8%	5.3%
Δ		1.4%	-0.7%	-0.5%
afe_ID_84	3.6%	3.2%	3.2%	3.0%

Table 11 (Own illustration): Comparison of forecast errors, days to expiry and trading volumes between real- and play-money markets.

Source	SS	df	MS
Model	.116171192	2	.058085596
Residual	.345663378	666	.000519014
Total	.46183457	668	.000691369

Number of obs = 669
F(2, 666) = 111.92
Prob > F = 0.0000
R-squared = 0.2515
Adj R-squared = 0.2493
Root MSE = .02278

fe_id_82_84	Coef.	Std. Err.	t	P>|t|	[95% Conf. Interval]	
av_id_82_84	-8.75e-06	5.93e-07	-14.76	0.000	-9.92e-06	-7.59e-06
d_id_82_84	.000226	.0000352	6.42	0.000	.0001568	.0002951
_cons	.0759099	.0032186	23.58	0.000	.06959	.0822297

Table 12 (Own illustration): Multivariate regression of forecast errors (FE) against aggregated trading volumes (AV) and D (days to expiry) for real-money (82 & 84) contracts on currency exchange rates.

Source	SS	df	MS		Number of obs	=	2403
					F(2, 2400)	=	175.44
Model	3.60657461	2	1.8032873		Prob > F	=	0.0000
Residual	24.6684323	2400	.010278513		R-squared	=	0.1276
					Adj R-squared	=	0.1268
Total	28.2750069	2402	.011771443		Root MSE	=	.10138

fe_id35_39	Coef.	Std. Err.	t	P>|t|	[95% Conf. Interval]	
av_id35_39	-1.38e-06	1.18e-07	-11.72	0.000	-1.61e-06	-1.15e-06
d_id35_39	.0016048	.0003261	4.92	0.000	.0009653	.0022443
_cons	.2360395	.016324	14.46	0.000	.204029	.26805

Table 13 (Own illustration): Multivariate regression of forecast errors (FE) against aggregated trading volumes (AV) and D (expiry) for real-money (82 & 84) trading observations on currency exchange rates.

	D							
	-80	-70	-60	-50	-40	-30	-20	-10
all	14.5%	13.2%	12.9%	9.6%	8.9%	10.8%	14.0%	11.5%
play				6.6%	10.1%	7.8%	12.2%	9.5%
real	14.5%	13.2%	12.9%	11.2%	8.4%	12.0%	14.7%	12.3%

Table 14 (Own illustration): Multivariate regression of FE against AV and D for identical play (39 & 39) and real-money (82 & 84) contracts (both currency exchange rates, external, economical, indexed).

	D			
	-40	-30	-20	-10
contract ID 35	5.9%	5.3%	5.6%	5.7%
Δ		-0.6%	0.3%	0.1%
contract ID 39	16.9%	19.0%	20.7%	24.1%
Δ		2.1%	1.7%	3.3%
contract ID 82	5.1%	6.5%	5.8%	5.3%
Δ		1.4%	-0.7%	-0.5%
contract ID 84	3.6%	3.2%	3.2%	3.0%

Table 15 (Own illustration): Average Forecast Errors (AFE) of 10-day intervals (D) for play- (35 & 39) and real-money contracts (82 & 84) for indexed currency exchange events

	-100	-90	-80	-70	-60	-50	-40	-30	-20	-10
5	9.8%	9.6%	4.9%	4.0%	3.9%	3.8%	3.4%	3.3%	3.5%	3.4%
Δ		-0.3%	-4.7%	-0.8%	-0.1%	-0.2%	-0.4%	-0.1%	0.2%	-0.1%
1	23.5%	23.5%	23.5%	23.5%	22.9%	22.6%	22.4%	21.0%	19.3%	15.2%
Δ		0.0%	0.0%	0.0%	-0.5%	-0.4%	-0.1%	-1.4%	-1.7%	-4.1%

Table 16 (Own illustration): Average Forecast Errors (AFE) of 10-day intervals (D) for a binary (5) and an indexed contract (1): indexed contract yields excess accuracy.

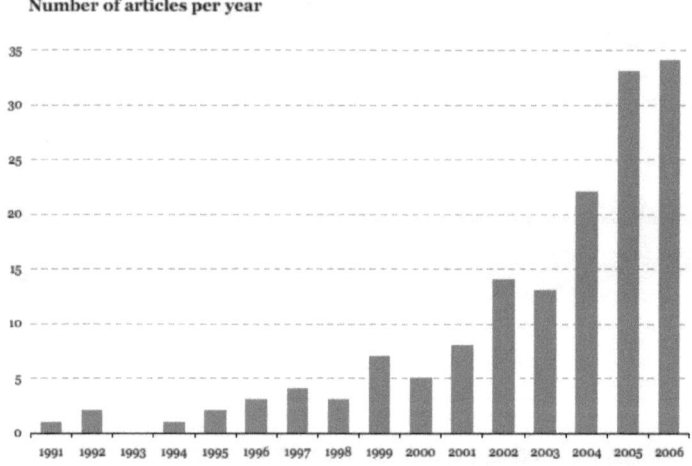

Figure 2: *Publication trend*

Figure 1 (Tziralis &Tatsiopoulos, 2006): Number of published articles in prediction market research between 1991 and 2006: Observable increase in academic focus.

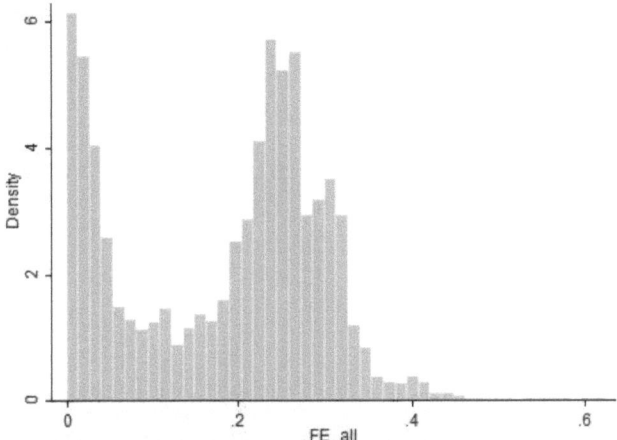

Figure 2 (Own illustration): Histogram of all observed forecast errors in trading activity: High density for trading activity at low forecast accuracy (market prices close to expiry value).

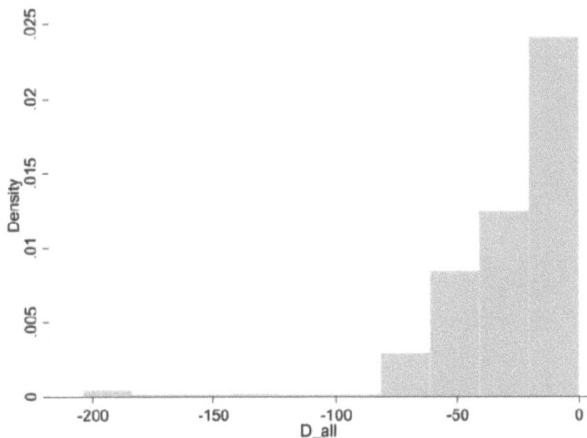

Figure 3 (Own illustration): Histogram of all observed days-to-expiry in trading activity: Negative correlation between D and number of trades.

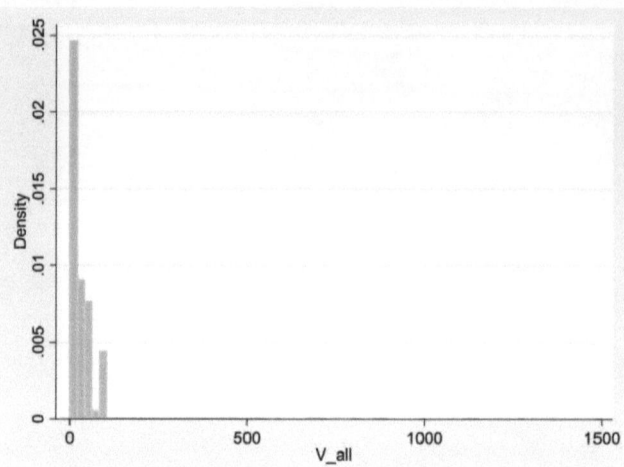

Figure 4 (Own illustration): Histogram of all traded volumes: High density for low amounts indicates high degree of risk-averseness.

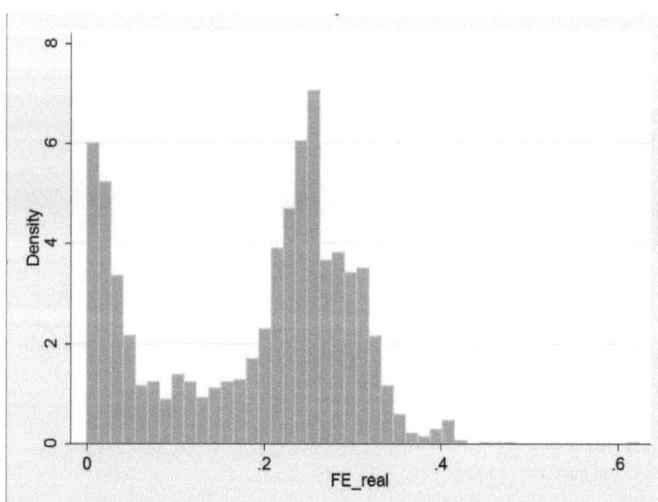

Figure 5 (Own illustration): Histogram of all observed forecast errors in real-money trading activity: Since N is substantially higher for real-money contracts no major deviations to FE_all are observable.

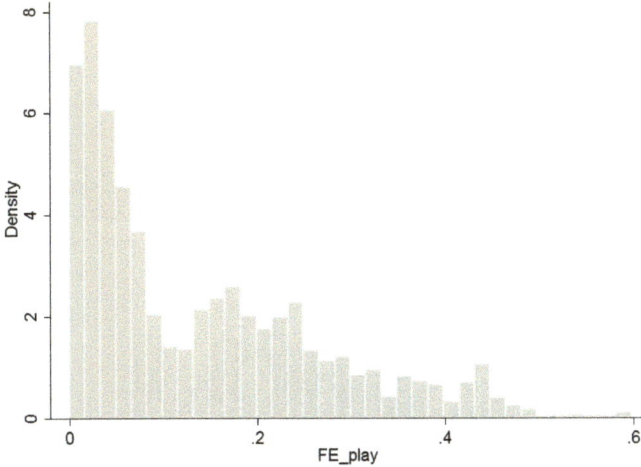

Figure 6 (Own illustration): Histogram of all observed forecast errors in play-money trading activity: Since N is substantially higher for real-money contracts no major deviations to FE_all are observable.

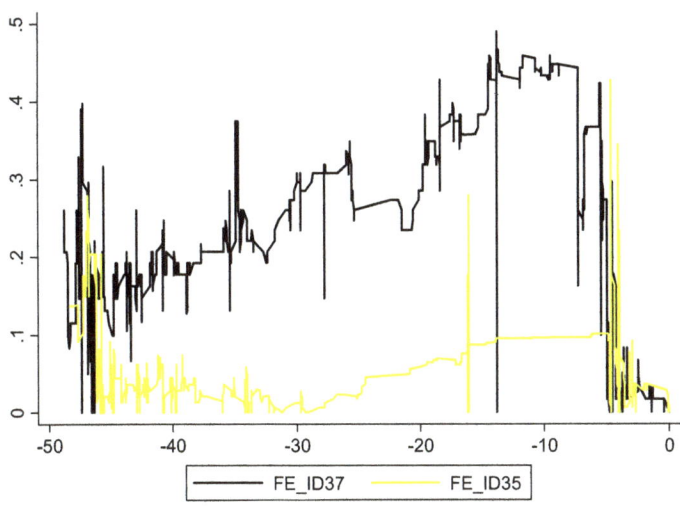

Figure 7 (Own illustration): Development of forecast errors (FE) in play-money contracts on currency exchange as days-to-expiry (D) approaches expiry

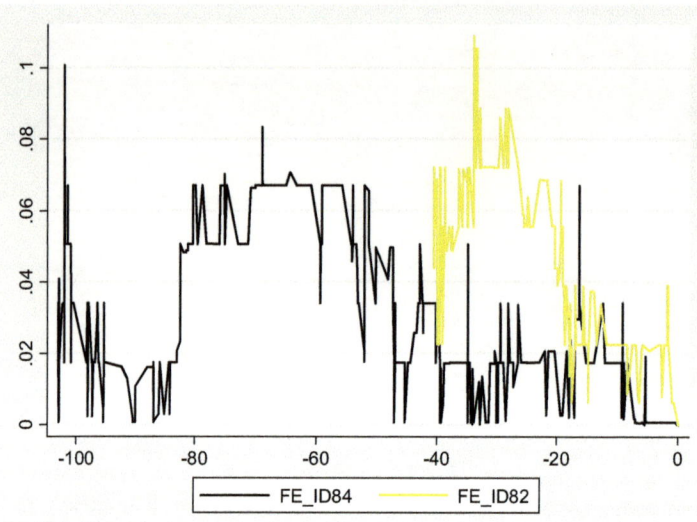

Figure 8 (Own illustration): Development of forecast errors (FE) in real-money contracts on currency exchange as days-to-expiry (D) approaches expiry

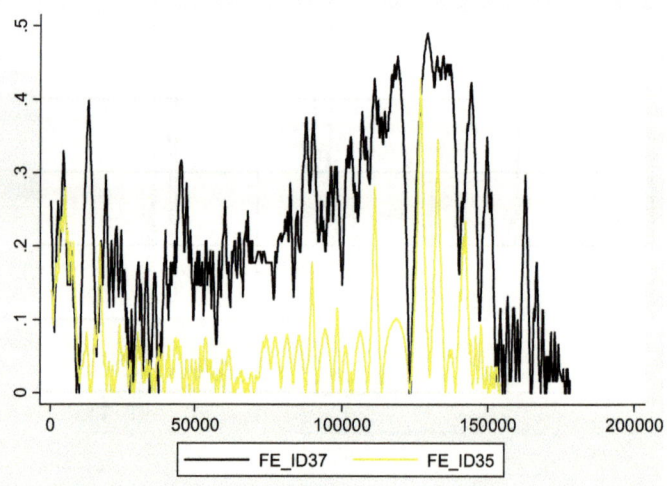

Figure 9 (Own illustration): Development of forecast errors (FE) in play-money contracts on currency exchange for increasing aggregated trading volume (AV).

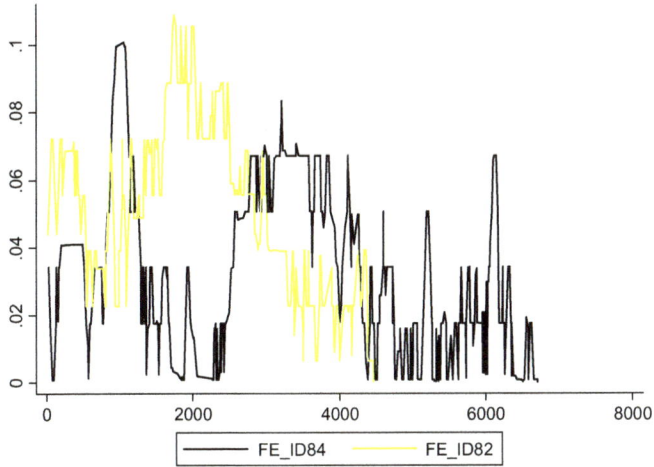

Figure 10 (Own illustration): Development of forecast errors (FE) in real-money contracts on currency exchange for increasing aggregated trading volume (AV).